SAY HER NAME

Say Her Name

ISBN: 978-1-7392546-6-7

Dark Thirty Poetry Publishing
First edition

Artwork by: Faye Alexandra Rose

DTPP17

DARK
THIRTY
POETRY
PUBLISHING

"Women will be hidden no more. We will not remain hidden figures. We have names. ... It was woman that gave you Dr. Martin Luther King, Jr. It was woman that gave you Malcolm X. And according to the Bible, it was a woman that gave you Jesus. Don't you ever forget it."

Janelle Monáe

It Still Happens

Siobhan Hickey

We took the shortcuts
And we didn't.
It still happened.

We listened to music
And we didn't.
It still happened.

We drank many drinks
And we didn't.
It still happened.

We said where we were going
And we didn't.
It still happened.

We wore what we were told
And we didn't.
It still happened.

We took to the streets in daylight
And we didn't.
It still happened.

It still happened.

It's
Still
Happening.

Nesting Doll

Amber Louise Horne

One day I bent over too far in skinny jeans.
It split me and left a seam around my middle,
just above my bellybutton. My torso fell
to the floor and where organs should have oozed
and erupted, I saw my younger self stood inside.
Her eyes closed almost like she was sleeping.
My legs were like high waisted trousers on her.
I called out from the floor, but she didn't move
so I balanced myself on my lower ribs and
pushed her over. She fell out of my legs and
cracked on the floor like an egg. Her fried white
hair spilling across the carpet. Amongst her lay
an eleven-year-old with a smile on her face and
wonky teeth. I walked on my hands to get to her
but she was so fragile that the moment my tired
breath landed on her pale skin she shattered
into a blushing six-year-old. Gangly in the flower
girl dress that she wore to her Dad's wedding,
I picked her up out of myself and held her
with a tenderness that has been lost for years.
I don't recognise myself in her anymore and yet
she fits into the parts of me I thought were buried
like fossil fuels. Her eyes are like oil spills.

Letter To My Future Daughter

Eleanore Christine

From the moment I first held you in my arms
I have known both love and fear
with every breath and every step you've taken
because I know what this world is capable of.

The eyes that leer and linger too long
reducing you to a piece of meat
devouring you like prey
the shadows that slink and stalk in the night
following too closely behind
the drug slipped into your drink
while you're in the bathroom.

My precious girl
I will do everything I can
to make sure you survive
I promise, I promise, I promise.

I will teach you to keep your keys
between your knuckles
to carry the word no like a weapon
like a sword at your side
how to be banshee and Valkyrie
to scream loud and fight back –

if they give you the chance.

But I weep bitter tears at the thought
that even if you do everything right
even if you are perfect

this still might not be enough
and a boyfriend could leave bruises
or a stranger could do worse.

And I want to howl until my throat bleeds
wolf woman, ferocious and feral
sharpen my claws and fangs
grab misogyny by the jugular
rip and tear and bite and break
bring the beast down
so I no longer have to tell you be careful
instead of be free.

A Woman's Worth

Elle Kehres

I am nothing more than a space holder;
The pause before a song's chorus
Or the tedious worldbuilding at the start of a
fantasy novel;
Just an idle hobby, truly;
A book to be set aside at any time.

How am I to know
That I am worthy of all the smiles,
Every cackle of delight,
When, as the sun sets in your eyes
I'm left awake wanting?

How am I to know
That each sharp turn of phrase,
Every inverted rainbow that tugs your lips
Down
Down
Down
Is not a reflection of me?
Of the heart I offer up on a silver platter;
The cherry on top of your preverbal sundae,
Quickly and carelessly devoured.

How often I mold myself to you;
To all my lovers, really,
A piece of clay smoothed to your liking;
Filling your cracks, making you whole,
While I'm lost in my lover's hands
As you shape me to your will.

It's never enough.
I'm never enough.
The grass is always greener.

And yet, I try.
Wrap myself in satin and lace;
Tied up in strappy heels,
In rope,
In lies,
Pretty as a package on Christmas morning
If you even deign to unwrap me.

If you even deign to love me.

For what is a woman
If she is not loved by another?
If she is not held up to the light and deemed valuable;
Another diamond, long succumbed to the pressure.

For what is a woman
If she is not revered as a mother?
If she ends the day alone;
Whispering softly to her plants
As she turns down the lights.

The garden of my heart withers a little more each day;
Each time I am passed over,
Like overripe produce on the grocery store shelf;
Each time I'm told goodbye,
Just another chink in your armor,
Another notch in your belt;
Each time I am left for another woman.

Am I still worthy
If I'm not lighting up a room?
If I'm not caught in a lover's embrace?
If I'm not your lucky charm;
A shiny penny flipped heads-side-up on the pavement?

I suppose only I can answer that question.

I'll Text You When I Get Home

Danielle Montgomery

I do the half-skip-walk past bus stops and alleyways
- every shadow is a hunter in waiting -

this is the suburban Serengeti and I'm a lost gazelle
wearing pepper spray perfume and faux fur armour

I see a shirt snagged on iron railings, picture a girl
lying in a grass verge with freshly mottled skin

a dog barks and I look for its owner, expecting a
wagging tongue to penetrate my mouth and
silence me

the sky creeps closer, pushing down on my head like
a thirsty boy in bed, i'm gagging on thick air -

walking home is a luxury
walking home is a sin
I shouldn't have drank
I should have got a taxi

I'm a piece of raw meat heading to the lion's den
they can smell the fear, taste my menstrual blood

I count my footsteps like clockwork and

pray I'm not preyed upon

the doorway swallows me whole...

"hey, I just got home xx"

Asymmetrical Lover

Roya Motazedian

Twist and turn me round and round
in their hands
try to find out why the left
doesn't match the right
discard me because I'm
asymmetrical
forget about me because I'm
replaceable
by something more intact
woman
always the second option
woman
always irrational
never makes sense.

high maintenance,
over-dramatic,
sensitive,
the synonyms of
woman
I almost bow my head
to avoid the limelight of their
male gaze.

there is no need
for me
to make myself legible
to you.

my eyes scream

feminist
and they cower away from me
men killer!
they holler
not knowing that
they make me wish I was dead
not them
I'd rather be buried
in their place.

I am
asymmetrical
none of me
makes sense
every part of me
illogical and mismatched
but somehow these parts still
connect together
and somehow women still
exist as they are.

Two Of Wands: I Will

Christina Hennemann

I'm holding the world in my hands on top of this mountain, and for what it's worth, I have the right to vote for freedom or shame, the power to bear gold or skin, the duty to speak silver truths. In this case, silence serves as compliance's sinister friend.

Man, it was so straining to get up here, centuries of fighters climbing the mountain, inch by inch creeping up. Now my feet are carried by their footprints on the smoothened rocks, my pores weeping for every slip of the foot, my hands reaching up as I'm sliding downhill.

I used to have two equal wands, my human right and privilege, my choices never feather-like, but free— will I have to travel to the moon now to marry my womb, embrace my Venus? The second wand is slowly fading, the Tarot card crumpling in my hands, red coal to ashes.

I'm still looking up at the tiny tinkling stars, each of them a spirit baby, patient and wise, telling me all they want is to be wanted. Control is a human fetish, they say, and they pray for us. I can't picture them thrown onto blood-stained soil.

A dark force grabs that hot second wand hard, from me, my sisters, my mothers and daughters, but we're holding on to both: we carve the wands in stone tablets, right here on this mountain, and they will stay here, closer to heaven, until we return from the dark valley of the night.

I Am But A Poem

Lisa Marie Serna

I'll do my best to explain.
Bear with me.
I only speak a thousand words;
I speak in lines and metaphors
I try to explain but
I pour out poetry-
Leaving you to figure out
anything more between the lines
because I, too, am trying
To figure out the conflicts inside
I'm not leaving that up to you.
Until I feel I'm no longer holding on by a thread,
Just take the words as my white flag
though it seems, in silence, I lollygag-
Know that I am trying to make it
Make sense for you,
I don't have to.
I wish you'd want to dive into me
Like I dove into poetry
Breaking down the possibilities
And meanings
Just taking
The poems for what they simply
but so diversely were.

Daemonslayer

Katie Ness

Light blazing like slaughter, a scorched creature
plummets from the Elysian sky.
Aphrodite foam tide brings bubbling blood.

Each memory of you is a cage and a dagger, my
cruel dark March boy. All your gloaming became a
raven's feather that sang through the keyhole,
splintering. The craving and the crush.

Scratched my cunt. Pierced me plenty into
silence. A cut throat, Piscean charmer.
A whirlpool swirling towards little oblivion, It
drained me down to the abalone.

Call to all the ghosts that haunt my bones. You
lived on, in there–a silver slipstream shroud.
Trap-door, gun-mouthed, Saturnian solar eclipse
slit my pretty Venus throat.

Lord of shadows and broken things. Your blade is
covered in my lunar blood; dripping.
You made the rains lover; creator of chains.
Sadistic cock, brute–tongued riled bitter tang!

Carcass of seas but speaks with the tenderness of
flowers.The lisp of poison in every memory, I
drank up every machete word. A parasite-addled
jackal mutilating these holy lights

But in my dreams the voice command is wild. A white hot earth howling! What Chthonic rage I've buried! In a space between my breasts, a diamond formed. Refracting shimmering lustre.

I ran fast into the forest. I am no longer your corpse-lover. I am the huntress! My songs are swords and scars and canticles of fury. This is the great devouring!

I stamped on that damn moon, I was tired of being *your* moon. Frail mothlight, breaking.
So I slipped her into my pocket like a coin until it's safe to shine again.

Twist the sinews, crack the cartilage and bind the bones into powder. Cut the tongue through the middle, stuff it with rosemary and rot. Pluck out your spiteful eyes. Peel away the past.

I eat each offering until the pain fades. I eat this death. I eat this hurt. I gorge on your violence. Crouching bird-like, hands cupped to feast on the broth of your briny blood.

What is left is a shrieking, shapeshifting, cursed thing grasping for the ruined sun, Kali glistens by the shore, a proud mother watching.

Justice sought can be ugly-fought. As true as my blooming and becoming. Another daemon slayed, a trinket for her collection, the wounding beaded like a pearl.

Shame

Bethan Keogh

In a cab.
On a dance floor.
On a bus.
In the metro.
A stranger's hand on my thigh,
In my underwear,
On my hip while his crotch gyrates against my back,
On my breast,
A ridiculous honking gesture,
That rendered no sound.
Just shame.

We Are Queen

Robin LeOra

She was shrouded with shade
A heavy gait in her walk
With shoulders curved and chin to chest.
An observer, she was not.
She had tired of that exhaustive
Frivolity many moons ago.
Alone, she was,
A nomadic wanderer through
Minds third eye...on the cusp of awakening.
Speaking to the resounded entity revered as...

Woman

Jeans with loose Tee or booty shorts with crop top
with Nike high tops to match
A room she commands
With the sleek blood red slip dress and darkened
stilettos showing off at their highest peak.
Maybe an oversized sweatshirt with knee-socks
that climb.. letting you know that regardless of
what's adorned... she will always be her own...

Prima Donna

Satisfied in the calm and quietude of her plucked
and picked surroundings.
Where she finds herself lost in the spine of words
and crisp pages of escape.
Here she learns and grows

whilst feeding the nodules of curiosity, desire, empowerment, and soul claiming...
where possibilities abound, stretch, and surrender to all that breathes within the rib-caging of this...

Enchantress

Lips tremble from tantric thrashings
Where thighs quake and hips flex
Sending Ivory dermis into prickled penetrative waves
Arches formed... ascending with mounds pressed forward
Where wisps of sun kissed tresses adorn
The dips hidden in the valley of pore seeping salted layers
Releasing their carnal essence and claiming her...

Queen

Surrounded by the elements of comfort
Heart full and free where young innocence
Finds safety and comfort within the bosom of
Maternal biddability
Here, tears are wiped from smudged dimpled cheeks And licked clean, forever gurgling within the belly Of this sin eater's labors, known as...

Mother

Curls and strands that now lack luster
Displaying wisdom of a journey endured
Represented in each graying tendril
In each calloused fingertip...that had tended
The trepidations of that which would've placed

Job on his knees in beseeching protest
An Aura felt across a gentle breath
A smile dipped in David's poetry...
Where we can now call her...

Goddess

And....
        I..am she
                You...are she
                        They...are she
We
    Are
        She

Metamorphosis

Sophie Watson

I.

They drink. They get drunker.
Men get uglier when they're drunker.

I drink their ugliness away.

II.

He drinks. He gets drunker.
His drunkness doesn't make him ugly, it
makes him smile. It makes him kind.
He steadies me with a hand on my elbow
asks if I want another one. *I'm at a good*
level, I say. *One more and I'd be throwing*
up.

Good, he says. I don't want you to be sick
I want you to be well. He is almost beautiful
To me then, under the piss yellow lights of
the pub. The next day, he writes me
Into a poem

And I feel it pulling at me.

III.

He doesn't pull me. I don't want to be
Pulled. I walk home alone through the dark,
unpulled. *What do they want from us?*

Woman-child, cynic

I think I know.

IV.

But do I? It's more than that, though.
It's more than the slip and slide of limbs
More than the *in out in out what's it all about*
of sex. He wants my image for his iconography.

He wants an image of himself.

V.

I want an image of myself that's worth more
than the image that he holds of me. But that's a
trivial truth. I'm no better than I ought to be.

I'm no better than him.

The Ossonoban Virgin And The Fish

Rebecca Gutteridge

Why is it they always throw away the women,
unless she is a bearer of sons,
a pure woman - an even purer paradox.
What hope is there?
When the Moors threw the Virgin
into the sea and were punished
with empty nets; a flurry
only returned when she was restored.

The first fish had a glass eye,
the fishermen's wives gutted and descaled it.
Discarded flakes shimmered
on the flagstones, and for a while,
they were important.

Why is it women are always restored
missing a part of themselves?
Or as icons,
anointed high above the rest
so that we can never touch her.

The Woman In Blood

Mimi Flood

The woman comes out of the far distance.
Nude, it's what you like to like but also deny.
But she's covered in blood.

People like to throw around traumatized. That fetus is a human
And experiences feeling, trauma.

A ten year old girl was raped by her stepfather and denied an abortion
Do you think she's traumatized? Do you think she will suffer PTSD?
Do you think she will scream at night? Do you think her back will
Crack, splinter with a sound of a crying baby from a far or near after giving birth?
Do women and young girl's rights matter? You want to have a debate? Our life isn't a
Debate. Our body isn't a law. Our life isn't a bounty. When we're born we are objectified,
Sexualized, and denied. We don't fall into the pit, we dive.

And when a woman comes out of the far distance.
Nude, it's what you like to like but also deny.
But she's covered in blood.
All the dogs got loose.

Running and hollering with open mouths.
If they were using their snouts

They would have known
It wasn't her blood.

(Un)becoming A Mother

Cara Pleym

What I expected least from my pregnancy was
resentment.
I longed to be a mother, replace the shame of
being a daughter with other,
new, unbruised and unblemished,
famished with hunger to love someone so deeply
that they would never doubt it.
Thing is, I knew it before the test lines divided my
life,
but I still poured that gin, didn't I?
Couldn't believe it, rejected it so thoroughly
that I couldn't understand these new cells were
part of me.
I wanted so badly to do it differently
but I framed this growth in my loss,
I wasn't ready, hadn't published, heating fucked
and boiler cold
and of all the boilerplate responses one is
supposed to have,
anger never rated. I felt so ashamed.

My identity was torn in two,
into who I thought I'd be and this feeling.
I broke down every day but with each came a
breakthrough,
a barrier dissolved as I resolved to overcome this,
be the mum I never had,
and this was my chance, wasn't it?

I booked an early scan,
I needed to connect with my child,

see her in black and white
but-
she was silent. Quiet for so long
it could only mean something was wrong
and I could sense her trying to frame it,
I held my breath,
waiting for her to tell me that my daughter was dead.
I was carrying a corpse
and she had passed a month before.
It should have been abhorrent.
Missed miscarriage, she called it.
I was strangely proud that I carried her for so long,
this was her home,
and the pills were never an option,
she could stay as long as she wanted.

I never understood motherhood until that moment.
Everything I had tortured myself with,
insignificant.
I realised my fear came from an abiding love,
that I didn't want to fuck her up
and in a cruel twist by that bitch mistress fate
I learned my lesson far too late.
With growth comes loss
but a different direction this time.
They warned me, I suppose,
the test even looked like a pause sign.

I can pour the wine now.
Spend the money freely.
But the bottle does not bear my new identity.
I am a mother.
I am a lover.

Friend, future,
an anchor for someone else.
Anchored by someone else.
Her death reformed me
and I have so much still to learn.
But god I wish it could be with her.

Exposure

Rebecca Gutteridge

It is 2 am on a Saturday – Storm Warning.
The international grid of masculine risk hums
through Town. 50 minutes until the 15 arrives.
No cabs.

A man has just exposed his penis to me

on Drury Street. Strange, how such a small and
feeble thing can engulf
everything else.
He looked triumphant -
spending a penny turned into
an opportunity.
I worry for a second he must be cold
standing there on show,
before I register
something untoward is happening.
Storm Eunice has exposed all four seasons in one
day
and trudging through sludge to home (it is 2 am
on a Saturday)

a man
has exposed himself to me.

Only I don't like the phrase "exposed himself".
Expose (external, exoskeleton, express, excite);
the word is unjust –too passive, too seductive, too
Netflix true-crime.

A smooth medley of consonant and vowel
(seductively feminine) but outsidedly masculine.
Expose.
It fails to capture the visual violence
of the unsolicited act – or the vulgarity of a penis.
It makes me feel like our collective terror too
often scripted into silence is euphemised down
to
nothing.

But I cannot shock my reader with too many
"penises" in one poem;
I do not want to be exposed in a bad light.

I wish I could laugh at him, unfurled out here.

Impossible; I am folding
in on myself, like empty Ikea boxes
that once housed almost-objects
ready for construction
being folded flat, ready for the skip:
regressing
into a small, defenseless child again.
There is something strangely fragile
about him too, I can't put my finger on it,
glazed and slurring

and holding himself in his hand. He is smiling at
me.
I do not even know his name – It seems strange to
ask the man with whom I am now intimately
acquainted.

My father told me once to scream "fire" in
situations like these,

thanks, Dad – I'm not surprised I ended up here
with advice like that,
I'll laugh about you later with friends
(our flasher stories, the silliness of men
dehumanising us)
and the wounds of womanhood, old and new,
will be salved a little. We will laugh
about how counterintuitive it is,
when faced with exposure
that I am carried away, (in the suspended
reality of an Orange Warning) like a dream,
to a lunch break in Year 1,
I remember it quite clearly:

the playground tyrant pushes over a little girl,
he smiles
                    down at her
like a little psychopath admiring
his handiwork as she works over
grazed knee with perplexed hand and begins to
cry,
unable to comprehend, through sniffles and sobs
why she was targeted
too young to be a receptacle of violence.
I wonder where he is now, if boy-handling girls is
a gateway crime

to man-handling -
or exposing a man's manhood indecently to
women?
Like a stranger just did to me.

Has that little girl, all grown up or perhaps even
earlier been forced to witness –

a stranger's genitals out-of-doors?

Did she keep it a secret? Did I make her up?
Perhaps being transported to playgrounds is
some creative trauma response. Freud would
probably say I have penis envy;
thank God my therapist is a Woman.
But Freud is right, I am envious;
he knows nothing of our fear, when she

registers the heaviness of his tread

in the dark, or at home and every cell stands on
end preparing her for flight – on a good day.
On a bad one, she is fastened down to hard ground
by the mortar of her sex,

by the improbability of her chances against him,

by the statistical scramble for survival recalled
from a pastel infographic:

fingering for keys
cabs
brightly lit escape routes
couples to cling to
trying to seize agency
where there is none to be found.
I am ashamed.

It is past 2 am on a Saturday. It seems darker
than before. The 15 has just driven past me.
Another 50 until the next one. I flick a finger;
some night bus.

Gale-force gusts have shaken the foundations
of our society today.

Met Éireann has issued a warning.
Eunice has blown the streets clean;
they are naked now
and we should all be afraid.

Pretty Girls

Carella Keil

In time, even the brightest stars will fade, dusty fingerprints left on felt black. It was a vain complaint, but she pleaded, "I don't want to be beautiful. Beautiful is for Impressionist paintings and sunsets, beautiful is cosmic explosions in the sky and the Auroral sheen of an oil-slick." Beauty is a force of nature; beauty makes you stare. Beauty is the edge of a razor-blade, a fine line between it and horror. Beauty cuts too deep, you can't hold its gaze for long.

"I just want to be pretty." Pretty girls will put a smile on your lips. Pretty girls never cause recoil. Pretty girls, delicate and non-subjective. "I just want to be pretty, like a memory cast in amber and firelight."

Samara's Pen

D.L. White

Samara grips a pretty pen
And commits fresh new crimes,
Ones which forbid the feminine
From writing verse or rhymes.

The paper isn't illegal,
Though made from slaughtered trees.
The pen isn't illegal;
A man can wield it free.

Guns in hellion hands,
They seem to break no laws,
And the theft of fathers land
Bears no punishment at all.

Violating her unripe body
Breaches no legislation,
But this pretty pen she holds
Dooms her to annihilation.

Suddenly her existence
breaks draconian rules.
Her, her pen and cursive
Enrages fiendish ghouls.

The poppy fields down the road
Are proffered military protection,
But her petals crushed unguarded
Under barbaric desecration.

Samara's mind now dangles
In hopeless choking smog,
All her dreams embezzled
By malignant marauding mobs.

Samara's pen is leaden now,
Until last week it feathered.
She used to fly through paper dreams
Which lie in ashen tatters.

Samara was the best in class
And showed such bright potential.
Now future mirrors mothers past:
An inkless, dreamless vessel.

"Education will set you free"
And for years it truly did,
But evil forced the teachers flee
The rest were left beheaded.

The languages she learnt
Can never pass her lips,
The books must be burnt,
Even her journaled scripts.

"The pen is mightier than the sword"
So says the cliched phrase.
In the rawness of the real world
Ugly weapons rule the day.

The shadows of oppression
Emaciate built up trust.
Jagged rocks of regression
Stone proud history to dust.

The beatings aren't illegal,

In forced matrimony.
The rape isn't illegal,
For she now belongs to he.

Samara smiles obediently
At her new disgusting husband,
She clings to prose and poetry
A risky secret contraband.

Hope slowly bleeds away
As the ink drips to depletion,
But words can't be contained
She keeps them in her conscience.

Thoughts without a canvas
Drive young minds to abandon.
She numbs painful haze away
With opioid medication.

Samara's pen runs empty now
The ink reduced to null,
She places it inside a drawer
And reaches for a needle.

Impact Statement

Nat White

"Hey. How are you?"

How am I? Was it not enough that your actions were so vile, I can only compare them to the bile that burns my throat each time my mind replays that scene?

Are you not satisfied, the force you used to gain control over me and my body, still grips my tongue in such a way, I cannot bring myself to speak your name? Fight every day to pretend that you do not and never did exist?

You want to know how I am?

As if the act weren't enough, you stained my future - in the same way you tainted me. Took advantage of my vulnerability. Slandered the sanctuary lining the walls of my home, left them screaming in shades of shame and disgrace.

You took something, that was never yours to take - then slipped into the shadows, as if it never happened [if anyone deserved to forget, it's me].

I owe you nothing.
Not my words.
Not my time.
Not my thoughts.
Not my forgiveness.

In just a few minutes you changed me in ways that cannot be undone, yet I do not seek revenge. You committed a crime for which no punishment by law nor deed will ever rectify.

You may think you have walked free. But just as you have left your mark on me - the spark that you sucked from my soul is evidence on your hands, you can never wash clean.

Until your last breath, you will know what you did, and you will have to live with it.

As do I.

Birth Of Power

Whitney Aumack

Be gentle, quiet.
Speak only when spoken to.
Meek, mild manner.
Bleed, but don't die.
Invisible lines, glass ceilings.
I hit harder than history.
My femininity isn't a crime.
So, I jumped from my ivory tower,
His jokes weren't very funny.
They said I was supposed to laugh anyway,
What is a man if not for his ego?
I landed softly in the movement.
Anger made me fertile; I became impregnated with ideas.
My screams echo as I birth my own power.
Swollen with intensity, one last push and a release.

Topic: HUMILIATION

Fatima Riaz

She held her mother's lukewarm hand
Crunched the brown autumn leaves
Under her small and dainty feet
With a tread that twitched every grain of sand
Fearlessly unaware of the beast
Who was after her life
The wolf romped around
Silenced her every sound
Brutally, her dignity shed
Her soul tearfully bled
The Earth wreathed in pain
The sky whimpered, she was plundered in rain
Helpless were the trees
Defilement brought life to its knees
There were tears in mother's eye
Who, along with her body, buried her heart
Trembling mourns depart
The ocean of agony will never dry
The clouds will always cry
When will such crimes be solved?
Pity to the angelic souls who get involved

Burn Down The Patriarchy

Eleanore Christine

For her hair, they took blood
and breath.

For a hijab worn too loosely
they arrested and brutalized her.

Left her to die in a hospital in Tehran
only twenty-two years old
because the government's morality police
likes to keep women on a tight leash like dogs –
Good girl. Stay, girl. Obey, girl.

Mahsa Amini, her death the matchstick
the ember igniting protests and rallying cries
of Zan, Zendegi, Azadi

Woman. Life. Freedom.

Six thousand miles away
my spirit aches with theirs
my sister souls who gather in the streets
far braver than I will ever be.

Who cut their tresses
in mourning, in solidarity
in defiance, in power.

Who remove their headscarves
and throw them onto bonfires
turning oppression into ash.

As if to tell the world
you cannot tame a lioness
you cannot put out the flame
that has grown into a blaze.

You must know by now
that what is fierce and wild
will always fight back.

Hear Me

Joely A. Serino

I interrupt people when they're speaking.
It's not something I'm proud of;
A flaw,
A shortcoming,
A problem.
I'm working on it.

But when you're the only woman in the room
where you have to wear a bulletproof vest
under your dress clothes,
When you're the only woman in the room
and all the darts are thrown at you,
When you're the only woman in the room,
stared down by your friendliest enemies,
You sit up a little taller,
And your voice gets a little bit louder,
And your words belt out a little quicker than
intended.

So I interrupt people when they're speaking.
I'm not trying to be rude.
I'm not trying to be first.
I'm not trying to be right.
I'm just trying to be heard,
In a room where
no one is listening.

The Girl Remembers Who She Is

Amber Louise Horne

On my shoulder sits a mark, a brand, a spot.
It cannot be outed. A match burnt till it scorched
my fingertips. Remember this feeling. A forgotten
life was lit like smoke reigniting a candle.
I let my head drift under the dreaded waters
of memory. Pull the thread of this pin pricked spot
to a lithe body that blackens and burns too
brightly
to be a metaphor. I burn and scream and writhe,
and remember my lungs engorged with water
that has sat for centuries. They cleansed me in
grit
and sediment and riverbed. This is when I marked
the spot, where I took a fingertip stained with ash,
and spotted white from sizzling fat and skin.
Where I
took the dirt and mud, bleeding from broken
fingernails
that clawed at pebbles and reeds. I took that pain
and burned a promise into my shoulder to
remember
that my mother made the candles for their wives.
That the lake water was once where they cleansed
their babes. I should have known that my funeral
spot would lie beneath their ceremonies. I Burn
and bite, knowing I am a woman, remembering
that I am not alone with my white candle heart.
I'll melt this wax into clean water. Soothe my
singed fingertips. When my mother broke her
waters

she trailed silver fingerprints along my skin and
this spot is not black and damned, it is onyx.
My body crackled, spat and burned. I remember
her.

Funeral Party

Claire Thom

The black widow,
leading a thread of crisp, clean suits,
watched as the flames ate the pinewood.
He was finally gone.
Ashes to ashes,
dust to dust –
she puts him neatly on the shelf.
Now who´s stuck in a box?

She yanks up the shutters
of eyelids, forced shut for far too long,
and grabs this fresh light.
She dusts off her brain cells,
locked in a cell for far too long,
and sweeps away cobwebs
that entangled her ambitions.

She winks at the clocks face
and grabs time's outstretched hand.
Time on her hands, finally.
Her life before tidied away,
along with the albums of mundane memories
and boxes of chores and routine.

She polishes the boredom from the mirror
and reveals a sparkling reflection.
She reflects on this image
of an old stranger before her.
Before him
and his story–

what was her story?

She irons out the crisp, clean paper.
Now there are no more
crisp, clean shirts to iron,
only this bold, blank page.
Inky waters begin to race
down transparent flumes
and words shoot out in splashes
of liberated creative power
and joyful triumph.

Hairstyles

Bethan Keogh

I was 15,
between two perfume ads,
an article gave me tips on how not to get raped
from the mouths of rapists.
Because it's important to stay young and pretty
and smelling like roses
and not raped.

One described how he grabbed women with their
hair tied up
or was it down,
I can never recall.
Sometimes I think of it as I tie my hair up on a
walk,
But since I'm never really sure which way was
deemed ok,
it's a useless tip.

Maybe if I can remember one day,
I'll take a walk and feel safe.

The Y Chromosome

Mimi Flood

I once read a man felt a woman's vagina
Was so close to her anus that it
Was displeasing to him and that
Her confidence and ego should be shattered
For thinking they're all that.
I once read a man felt a woman could control
Her period so when his coworker said she
Needed to go to the bathroom he said she
Could control all of that maybe set it aside till
About noon. I once read a man was in euphoria when
He would follow women to scare them
Without actually stalking them. But was.
Do you know nipples develop in the womb
before embryos become distinctly male or
female so by the time a Y chromosome
Kicks in to distinguish a fetus as male, the
nipples have already secured their place
So they never had a chance to become
A female in the first place. But you were pretty damn close.

The Canvas

Christina Hennemann

I'm spread out before you butt naked
and wait for your brushes to paint me;
Product description stapled
to the corner of my frame:
Raised as a girl to become a woman.
People pleaser, projection screen, poser.

Part your lips, chin down, chest out,
can you arch your back a bit more?
Fix her hair over there, smooth her dress,
let me adjust the bra strap, it's okay if I touch?
Perfect, click, beautiful, click-click,
look at the camera, seduce me,
yeah, that's it, we got it.

Talent, I ink on my hands,
street smart on my ass cheeks,
paint a purple pentagram as the heart,
fix a loaded barbell across my deltoid.
A girl's frail hand pencilled in the corner
where canvas meets frame, ducking—
Handle with care.

Hangnails

Carella Keil

Originally published in Open Minds Quarterly Vol. 19 Issue 1
2nd Place recipient in OMQ 15th Annual Brainstorm Poetry Contest

The girl with embers in her eyes
didn't always look
like this

She used to play in the sandbox
count the grains of stars
galaxies glistened on her knuckles

She slit open butterfly cocoons
dreaming nectar kisses
whisper soft as dandelion seeds

She hooked words together like magnets
screamed to make you listen
wore braces
over her smile

She smoked on curbs and
flicked ash in your face
at night slept in trees
head flung back limbs wrapped tight
leaves shaking
free

She used to soak the hate in under her skin

Now she runs her fingers over bark
just to feel the splinters

Eros

Sophie Watson

Your voice in my ear on that
Drafty night bus back to Europe
Filled me with sudden warmth and
I felt *oh no* like a sunbeam
You were (you informed me)
Making a curry

I'm in trouble.

Strange how we fool ourselves
Isn't it? You were in trouble.
I was trouble. I was basking in it
Like a shark in the gulf stream
Bathed in a light that seemed to
Dry up when I saw you waiting for me
When I got off the number 11.

Unobjectionable, hair a little
Flattened by the rain, you waited
With your nice face and beloved voice
A little higher than usual
Because you cared
and I loved you then with
A sister's tenderness
Because I knew that was all I'd ever love.

Still we persisted
Whether out of kindness or cruelty
I let you put your arm around me
Then (when you called me pretty)

I complimented your curry
And said that I liked your soul.

I wasn't lying. That means so
Little to you though. What strange
Creatures we must be, that with all the
Ways we know to love
Neither one of us will ever satisfy
The other. Shall we blame it on some
Trick of my pheromones that makes
Yours smell too sharp or sweet?
Or shall we simply find the other
Wanting? That's the problem.
When you lunged at me on the
Way back to the number 11
And blamed it on a romantic moon

I laughed a little higher than usual.

I Am Woman

Sana Mujtaba

History knows my name
As a warrior, obliterated and depleted
A sidelined narrative from the ghetto
Smoked serenity
As sands of time swallow my pride and Removed me from the throne of love
Wrapped me in thousand layers of dust
Placed me in the dungeons of dismal past
History knows my name
As the resilience of auburn skies
The ferocity of viridescent spirit sprouting from the earth during falls
My roots are ancient
For millions of years,
My voiceless dew drops danced with the sombre moonbeams
My muse
Running in the wastelands of desires
Lonesome found me and caressed me
The absence of the kindred spirit
The fraction of my decaying soul
Made me into who I am
I bear truth and smiled with sewn lips
Endured extinction of holy rains
Thirst for existence pushed me to extremes
I survived the venom injected into my streams
I withstood the burning venus suns
I will stay here until you are gone.

I Have

Elle Kehres

Have you ever stopped to watch -
And I mean really watch -
the way incense burns;
Dancing, curling and unfurling
Its smoke into still air?

I have in the same way I adore lost coins on busy streets;
Always sure to turn pennies "lucky" side up,
Wishing well to whoever may stumble across them next.

It's in the way I lean back to admire cotton candy clouds
And the circus of animals that keep me company high above;
Laying in the sweet summer grass,
Wind whispering in my ear.

It's how I will stop to wrap my arms around a tree trunk
As if it were a long-lost friend;
The scent of the wood a word on the tip of my tongue,
Its crackled bark beneath my fingertips.

It's why I stop to appreciate every grocery store bouquet
And find the time to acquaint myself with every scented candle;

Seeing what I might fit into my little universe.

It's the way an old book can feel in your hands;
Pages rustling like falling leaves, and why I always look for inscriptions
On the inside of each cover;
Longing to know what truths the story granted its previous owner,
And what messages were worthy of being passed on –
To a friend, to a lover, to those who share the same spirit I do.

It's in the same way that wilted roses make me wistful;
And why an old river makes me sentimental;
Knowing it will never be the same; always evolving,
A lone traveler, snaking its way through the forest floor.

Have you ever dined by yourself;
Tucked away in a corner booth
With just the menu for company,
Simply observing as the world spins on by?
Not exactly lonely, but awed. Reverent even.

Do you create intricate backstories
For each person
Sitting adjacent to you on the train;
Of the lives they might lead
Outside of these fleeting moments together?

Do you think nice thoughts to those
Speedwalking across the street?
Late.

Always late;
Lukewarm lattes precariously caught in a death grip.

When you're flying through the inky-black sky
Do you look down at each and every speck of light,
Illuminating each and every windowpane,
And marvel
At how many stories are playing out just beneath you,
Nose pressed to the glass?

Have you ever traced the freckles on a lover's arm,
Creating the cosmos right there
For both of you to share;
Finding meaning in the little spaces in-between?

I have. And I hope I never stop.

Untitled

Stefanie Briar

War has no justification.
NONE! DO YOU HEAR ME?!

It is a sickbed collective
of toxic, damaged men
banded together by false entitlement
and blind to their own humanity
because they were taught not to express it
(except for anger),
the only emotion they rebranded
as "acceptable to show",
because they were poured power
when hungry for love.

They are so desperate for healing
that march in uniformed unison
yelling battle cries of a shared cause
to feel like they belong.
These damaged humans
remain a hairsbreadth away
from cold metal machines
that allow their fragile fingers
to dole out the end of the very thing
gifted to them by a woman
like those clutching crying children
to their desperate chests,
hearts hummingbird-wing fast,
naked fear battling defiant courage.

I am each of those women,

wild-eyed with a scream that
could kill you dead where you're standing,
seeing my own child in the body
of every child lost
to soulless men across the world,
seeing ourselves in every woman cut down.
Our righteous rage
blows the roof off the atmosphere,
universe-deep and black as pitch,
trying to hold the evil of this world
above the ground
where no one sleeps soundly.

Can you feel it in the rain?
Can you hear it in the dropped bombs?
Can you see it in the rubble swallowed up by dust?
The anger of every woman
screaming in silent unison
to hex the hearts of every man
who chose allegiance to country
to money
to oil
to blood
to everything but love.

Fuck the patriarchy.
Fuck their power trips
and Putin's tiny dick.
Fuck war.
Fuck guns.
Fuck greed.
FUCK EVERYTHING that is evil!
FUCK EVERYTHING that is not peace!

Integrity

Lisa Marie Serna

Swollen eyes
Sleepless nights
Beauty products to disguise
The mismatch of hues
Brought on by the blues
And you show up, smiling.
Darling, you keep hiding
All of it so wonderfully.
you're not afraid to tell
the world you break
over and over again, too..
nor are you afraid
to show up and dress up
post-panic attack
when your bones want nothing
but darkness and rest
But there you are;
wholly you.

Reign

Sara Sabharwal

Wild woman
Magic woman
Woman made of star
Never forget how powerful you are
The world will try to strip you
Of the magic in your veins
Society will try to trick you
Out of what you want to say
Misogyny stains
A scarlet letter
Upon our pain
Our hope begins to wane
Like the moon in the sky
Do not let your light die
The spark within your heart
Is enough to start the fire
That will burn
Stop the world from turning
So that we may stop yearning
For the security we crave
The respect we deserve
We are not here to serve
As pawns in the patriarchal game
Rising up as warriors
We will not cave
Sisters made of stardust,
Now it's our turn to reign.

Nevermore

Lisa Marie Serna

From what I've seen,
I only regret the nights I didn't choose me-
The time I didn't get up to sing
even with my cracked vocals for karaoke-
The evenings I didn't get up to dance
And the trips I did not take-
stressing over a savings
that never made me save anything
Other than wonder and what ifs.
And thinking now, if or when the world
should crumble down
would all I have left
Is a checklist of unchecked
recipes, places, people and activities
I'll regret to have missed on this
adventure by stressing over
what was beyond my control –
actions that broke my heart,
Haywire politics, illness
and judgmental comments...
Things that have made me choose all
but
the risks-

never more.

Shakled

Cara Pleym

bring back the lightning strikes, the blindingly
annoying
middle of the night or start of a shower,
an overwhelming calling lyrical and light in your
blood
and you need to capture it now now now.
but now?
I colour my hair after sun and maybe that's why
the moon is pissed so the tides no longer haunt
me
and is that because I discovered ocean floors?
are they scared I'll spill their secrets
like I haven't learned the cost
of betraying an altar sacrifice?
cannot I both?
polarity, duality, it's in my very name
but what if I have no more truth to tell?
or I don't understand it, can't explain it
and so I can't leash it into words for you.

I step out, slapped back, too upset, a distraction.
who I am to me and for you is the difference
between salt air and entombed
yet I still can't bear to lose that.

the shiny preppy pretty wholesome selfless giving
girl
martyred and mated to your every wish.
all I've ever been is what's wanted,
conflict roiling and rebelling

and do you have any idea what's it's like
to slake someone's thirst when you hate them?
while you obey them?
sub on demand and god forbid I try
something new without your blessing.
I'm scared I need to be struck
just to shake something loose,
am I only capable of response?
injustice so ingrained
that it's the only way I know how to do it?
everything I like is tied to a memory
like it was fated.

But fuck that, fuck faking til I learn to like it
because you treat me better in the clothes you
picked out.
do you know how long I've waited to get tattoos
because of the disapproval?
like my very skin is owed but judged if too on
show
because I need to be whole and dirty just for you,
not sexual, not special,
just a blank page for your mess,
for me to reflect.

and that's it, isn't it? my pretty blue eyes
coloured only by the light outside.
maybe that's why I need to red so bright.

it's undeniable.

A China Doll

Amber Louise Horne

I lay at your feet in pieces.
My face splintered
down the middle.
The tip of my pinkie finger
has rolled to the doorway.
A penny sized chunk
of my bottom lip
sticks out of your flesh
just between the knuckles.

You wince,
pick out the shard and walk away.
My eyes roll back and forth
in my head like a china doll's.
Glossy, polished and utterly replaceable.

I sit up,
collect myself and
grab the superglue.
I find my big toe under the sofa.
An earlobe in the shaggy rug.

As I walk out,
I try and keep quiet,
keep my joints from
rubbing in their sockets.
Try not to creak,
and squeal.

Even if that's all my body can do.
I will be perfectly quiet for you.

Dragon Queen

Katie Ness

Ovoo. Thunderbolt beauty.
An arrow of the borderlands.
Opalescent dash across the void like a sun
catcher.
Sky rider, water weaver. She brings the rains.
A veil of comet-tailed rain, star speeding, Orion
leaping.

A soul of old, horns of velvet,
Eyes of emeralds in the milky bloom,
With serpent stealth and a jaguar heart.
Lady of the largest heart.
Her Jupiter tongue sang mantra to the
mountains.

There's a few left of her kind,
She bites the cage of life, unbound my Venus body,
Lifted me out of this sea of grief and storms.
Said 'ride with me' and took me on a journey
through this dreaming universe.

With snow in my hair like ritual feathers,
I became a dragon rider, the honour of a queen.
Ovoo soaks me in soft white gold,
My serpent maiden, her breath a song of springs.
A fair cry to the ospreys, her gaze severe as
summits.

Lovely is this noble lady,
Swerving across purpling moors to an opaline sea

We glide like gods in cloudnight,
Sailing in the stratosphere, dragon queen of twin blue
I chant her name Ovoo...Ovoo...Ovoo

Falling up into the stars, she shines like silver thread
Stitching into cobalt pool of moth light
Her voice brushes galaxies, looping through the ocean of milk
A crystalline pearl of laughter whirs through the waters
Purring a low gentle rumble, we dart, horizon born.

Untethered and unshackled I raise my hands with joy
Swift and strong and stable Ovoo shifts with the shape of birds
billowing petroglyph summons the shrine in apricot groves
Fountains rise, she gleams in the roses.
A temple of moon moths and butterflies.

I place a candle on the altar to the queen of heaven
Inscribe my name upon secret scrolls,
'My dragon rider, dragon queen' she says 'worthy of the throne'.
Ovoo, rain empress wash my past away,
Saint Maria's prayer, the daemon slayer,
She's fighting fire and churning gold by the sea.

Consent

Jillian Calahan

Consent
Noun: permission for something to happen
or
an agreement to do something.

But we aren't here to talk about
what consent is,
because you damn well know.
Here's what consent isn't:

Consent is not
a short skirt and cleavage.
Consent is not
bedroom eyes or exposed thighs.
Consent is not
the red wine stain on her lips.
Consent is not
laughing at your jokes.
Consent is not
a phone number.
Consent is not
a strip club lap dance.
Consent is not
your erection.

Consent is not
dinner and a movie.
Consent is not
a relationship status.
Consent is not

a wedding ring.
Consent is never forced.

Consent is not
how many men she's been with.
Consent is not
nakedness.
Consent is not
a sleepy yes
a drunk yes,
a stoned yes,
a drugged yes,
a coerced yes.
Consent is still not consent
if a yes is followed by a no.

And that goes for men as well.
Because men say no too.
Men feel pressured too.
Men get raped too.
Men deserve consent too.
Men consent.
Men consent.
Men. Consent.

Consent isn't free.
You pay for it
with respect and understanding.
If you can't afford it
you don't deserve it.
No means no.
No exceptions.
If you can't get that through your head
then maybe a bullet will.

Five

Eleanore Christine

Instead of a sanctuary, he turns their house
into a prison, appoints himself warden
keeps her in solitary confinement
isolated from family and friends.

Instead of I love you, he tells her she is stupid
she is a bitch, she is a whore, she is worthless
she is nothing.

Instead of tender kisses, he takes what he wants
ignores her cries of **no** and **stop.**

Instead of flowers, he brings home a pistol.

Like salt rubbed into open wounds
the judge decides that an object
deserves more protection than a human being
that his right to possess a firearm
is more important than her right to live
her epitaph signed with the bang of a gavel –

a survivor sentenced to become another statistic
five times more likely to be killed
when her abuser has access to a gun.

This cold and hard and metallic truth
is the deadly reality of being a woman
in America.

I Am A Woman

Jillian Calahan

I am a Woman.

I am more than my uterus.
I am more than just a time capsule.
Born of the past
and holding the future
in my belly.
I am a Woman.

I am more than my hips.
I am more than an hourglass figurine.
I am less curves and more cliffs.
These edges were not made
for anyone elses hands
but were sharpened for those
who just cannot help themselves.
I am a Woman.

I am more than my vagina.
I am more than your personal
playground slip n' slide.
I am more than just a portal
for your pleasure.
My pleasure matters too.
And my hands know
just where to find it.
I am a Woman.

I am more than my cervix.
And it's spelled C-E-R-V-I-X

not SIR-VIX.
So you can keep your man-made laws
out of and off of my body.
I am a Woman.

I am more than my clitoris.
You would know that
if you could find it.
I am a Woman.

I am more than my labia.
So when I say "read my lips"
I'm not talking from my hips.
Maybe it's time we change that phrase
to read my teeth.
I am a Woman.

I am more than my ovaries.
I am more than the hormones they carry.
The same hormones that make me
such a raging bitch
are the same hormones of my arousal.
You don't get to hate them half the time
and fuck them the other half.
I am a Woman.

So when you look at me,
what do you see?
A baby factory?
A pleasure center?
A housewife?
A whore?

Or do you see Me?

I am a Woman.

If you see anything less
then you are blind.

We Have Plenty To Be Angry About

Bethan Keogh

I don't walk up to them in the middle of the street.

Just to say 'ha! have you heard,
gay marriage is legal here now,
I think it's brilliant that a gender neutral toilet is
available at the cinema down the street.'

Just to argue the toss about human rights and
how people are people and how penguins are gay
so why can't your son be?

Just so that I can vent,
release a little bit of anger.

But God knows, we have plenty to be angry about.

Clockwork

Christina Hennemann

I fear nothing under the eye
of the moon

lunatic cycle over menstrual
cramps clots cleanse

the cup sucking at my walls like
strawberry mash

ovulation; I'm pretty fierce and
you're a sucker for love

you swing your magic wand—
inexorable waddling tail

I've seen them all before; my eyes
cold and white as the moon.

The Flower

Dawn Vincent

Oh, thousands have stepped the same path as this glorious plant
over the course of its life.
When seeded, it took ugly root
then grew beautiful.

Appreciated, but untouched,
it stayed healthy.

The winter lets it nestle safe under soil.
Spring comes
and it blossoms once again.

It blooms
and so
you assume
that it's for you.

You pull at the root
split the stem
and never will it be the same again,

You can try to revive-
to breathe in some life
but it is far too late
and even in the heady bright of day
she will never see another hopeful May.

And as such

you toss her, unflinching, onto grass, where she lays,
beauty ripped away.

You have nothing to say
but you suppose that you are not to blame.
The flower was yours to take.

She would have lasted forever,
through countless storms and bad weather,
but you could not resist, blamed your instincts
and the way that she looked -
and as you took her,
she was trained not to flinch.

Skinny Dipping

Carella Keil

Originally published in Dipity Issue 1

it was night
when we got there
and the sand shone like a million galaxies beneath
my
bare
naked toes

i tread upon a beach of venus
not really, the lake just beyond the city where the
highways are black strips of reality
our roads within the sky
you took me out here
the naked outdoors
it was so black i could not see your eyes
only the thousands of galaxies overhead
and below

where the night merged with the water and
everything became
one
shining black crater of the universe

our bodies in the spinning spools of galaxies
the water like the black sap of life
it trickled over my wet body

liquid stars breathing into me
i shuddered
treading

so
close
with you.

Beautiful Creatures

Fin Brennan

If I was me
I would never know how lucky I am.

I am me.
But I still don't know that.

I walked in the Big Smoke once
The world was wonderful back then.

The world is different there too.
As a small, big city boy I should be well informed.

I see them everywhere.
These creatures of mystique

To call them that in a loving way is all I intend
I trust they know that.

When you look at some
You turn to stone

When you smell some
You faint in euphoria.

When you talk to some
You don't say a word.

When you taste them
That's when you know they like you too.

Whore

Hannah Cross

Man's biggest prize,
Woody sheets wrapped neatly in flimsy plastic,
Fluctuating numbers flicker across a screen,
Glows in the glassy eyes of a pallid face,
Yet bestowed onto her for what?
Feigned intimacy and a piteous release,
Legs spread to reveal a discarded jewel,

They fought for her prized thing,

This thing that beats with the rhythm of a battle cry,
Not this useless body,
This depleted shell,
But her freedom,
It was won by a dead woman,
Laid lifeless before a stallion,
Her most prized possession,
Never to be parted with,
Lingers in the dank light,

But still he takes it from her,
In back alleys and marital beds,
Smothered screams and silent sobs,
She buys his treasure with the thing he snatches,
He never knows,
Never realises that it is him,
Who whores his emerald paper,
For something she cares little for,

His soul is heavier,
While his pocket rests lighter on trembling thighs,
Dirty,
Degraded,
She laughs at how easy he was,
How fickle,
How quickly he will part,
With man's biggest prize.

I've Just Had A Baby

Danielle Gilmour

I've just had a baby
Will you not remove your shoes?
Wash your feet?
This is holy ground
Watch you doff your cap as you approach my
throne
Bow your head
Lay palms where I tread
Please speak in more reverent tones

I am Lucy— honour the mother of mankind
Here, I'll show you what to do—
Kiss your fingers and touch your navel
Light a thousand candles, cast me a circle
Bring me offerings, keep my vigil

Do you think I willed this baby into being?
The least you could do is pour a libation
For the blood I've spilt and that flows from me still
Trace my sacred scars and name them a
constellation

I am Elastigirl— my heart and parts have
s t r e t c h   e   d
Beyond recognition
Even to myself

I am Eos— where is my golden chariot as I bring
you this pink new dawn?
And just moments before, I was Athena, roaring

as I rode to war

Where is my chapel among those raised
For every temple built within a body— cradled in pelvis or hidden by ribcage—
To hold our babies however long they stayed?

I am the Earth
I am the Sun
I am Wonder Woman
I am my mother and yours who allowed us to breathe

I've just had a baby
Walk backwards as you leave

You Should Be Able To Walk Home

adam Shove

All I can say to this is I'm sorry,
I'm sorry that we live in a world
Where this happens to women on a daily basis.
I shouldn't be getting phone calls
From each of my sisters
Or my friends worried that someone is following them
And can I pick them up.
It's not that we should have progressed,
Because we should never have been
At this place to begin with.
I never lived with any men
Until I was well into my twenties,
And I find myself apologising for a gender
That is very alien to me in terms of ethics
And stance of women's rights.
Every woman knows someone
Who has been sexually harassed or assaulted,
Very few men know of a man
Who has been the perpetrator,
And I don't understand why.
Nobody wanted to be the one to ask
Mephistopheles for help,
Because that would mean selling out.
The patriarchy would rather not have a change
To the status quo,
For rich white men replace those in power
Which were old rich white men.

This isn't the time we're living in,
It's the time we're subjected to.
We can't make a better tomorrow
Without acknowledging what is wrong today.
Again all I can do is say I'm sorry.

Fawning

Ashley Roncaglione

His shadow grows as he makes the descent
the fawn in the grass remains ever so still

Touching her body without her consent
in silence she lays though against her will

Forcing his fingers so impossibly low
she is but for sport and the hunter's thrill

He marks her forever with piss in the snow
wide-eyed she stares as he moves for the kill

March With Signs

Laura Bickford

Docile and weak
You see me as meat
You tell me to smile more
As if there is something
To smile for.

You question my strength
My wit and knowledge
You write us as stupid,
Afraid and quiet.

But we stand united
Hand in hand
We chant with signs
We all demand.

To be heard and be seen
As equal
And human.

I am a woman
And so,
I will stand.

For our daughters
Who should not
Have to walk
With signs and chant
To the man.

To My Future Daughter Part Two

Cara Pleym

I have learned that love is not unconditional.
It is not automatic or eternal despite my best
efforts.
It is one of the few things in life that has a low cost
upfront,
it is easy to fall in love.
The payment will come in ways you do not expect
and they hurt all the more for it.
A comment cruel and casual,
a dismissal,
or deadening silence when your mind is full of
fear.
To allow someone so close is to give them power.

I hope, my darling, that you give love as freely as I
once did,
and in that, you will be my daughter.
I hope you fill halls with raucous laughter,
and throw your head back careless and free
- mind the wall though, that fucking hurts.
I hope you show your heart to the world
but not all of it at once.
Let them earn it,
let them deserve it.
Do not waste your love
for I am sorry to tell you,
it is finite.
There will be a day when you run out,
when your pure and childlike heart
has no fucks left to give,

I'm sorry to say
you'll forget to forgive.

In all of this,
I hope that I love you
as I do now
and it will never be hard
and I'll reclaim that it's possible
to grow past the scars.
But I am sad and bittersweet
in ways which do not mix
and you'll test me – I know that.
After all, you are my daughter.
Your fury ignited will be stormclouds and lightning
and we'll battle on grounds of moral compasses
set to true north,
but we can't see them both.
But we'll learn.
With tea and toast of course.

There will be days when you cry
and it will be my fault,
there will be days when I die
because I've missed four calls.
So on the days where it's difficult
when bruised hearts are still,
I promise to love you,
for you I'll unbend my will.
We'll share sins over coffee
and you'll choke on a secret
and whatever you tell me,
I promise I'll keep it.
On all of the days
where you break my heart
I promise I'll stay,

I'll be here in the dark.

Of all the things I hope for
from every single wish,
God I hope you get to hear this,
I hope you exist.

Stilettos In The Rain

Carella Keil

Originally published in Shuf Poetry Issue 10

Seahorses with wings
can't decide between sky
and water
so stay on my mind.

Butterflies sleeping on telephone wires
candles melting in the rain.

Stilettos anticipate a long night
dancing to vodka lullabies.

Break This Cycle

Sana Sarfraz

Defined by our vagina
That's what we mean to you

A nice snug hole
To shove yourself into

A squeeze at the breast
Skin so soft and round

Dont forget the buttocks
Another place your hand is found

When you're all spent
Then ask us to make tea

Oh don't put your shirt on you say
Because you want to look at me

Now the endorphins are in your veins
You are all kind and sweet

Whispering honeyed words
And promising us treats

But it will wear off we know
The effect won't last long

The spell will soon be broken
Blood laced with venom's song

Your true self will emerge
With contempt and misery afore

With haunting words like lashes
And all unprocessed gore

But a dip in the vagina again
And all traces of menace gone

And here is the cycle my friends
Which goes on and on.

Marianne

Bethan Keogh

France is a woman.

Standing triumphant over men.
They are the spoils of war,
That carpet the ground.
Reduced to nothing but a bloody mound of limbs
and spines and layers of skulls and bones.

There's a tear in her dress,
delicate, freeing nothing but a single breast,
the whole pair would be too much.
Too provocative for the gaze of the men below.
For even up there, full of victorious in glory,
I'm sure she feels the weight of their eyes on her.

Svirajte Noćas Samo Za Nju (Play On Tonight Just For Her)

Dora Batinović

I did not run from home because the birds sang too loudly in the morning,
Or because the sweet honeysuckle of freshly mowed grass made me nauseous.
A momentary lapse in judgment, my naïveté preceded me;
my face a photocopy, my fate blueprinted eons ago.

Now that I've reached rock bottom, I believe in destiny,
like a withering leaf on an autumn tree.
Divinity squandered with the first breath—
stillborn by nature—
I never stood a chance.

I'm moving home.

I do not remember what my bare patted feet feel like among the blades of grass, or how much comfort I find in the smell of my mother's skin.
I do not have much of a sense of self—-my shoulders sinking deeper with each leaf turned—but to hear the birds sing, the sugary smell of June, and my mother's rampant chewing of sweet peaches seems like the closest I will get to forgetting my flesh.
Now I know why we shrink with age.

Even my hips give way and sway when whistled;
the shame swallows me from the thought alone...

Souring

Cara Pleym

Cherry flavoured safety
is tokenistic,
a ballistic missile aimed at blossom trees.

Artificially lit
in golden girls
flickering for deeper shaving shadows.

Duck egg fragility
in nobility
known for its flagellation.

Sire heathens from heather rock,
crush the scent for singing blood,
swallowing ash,
scimitar path.

You go first.
Tell me how it tastes.

To The Boy Who Took What He Wanted

Danielle Montgomery

you live in the curdled screams of my throat
where
thieves come for refuge - bloodthirsty
for a bite of innocence father forgot to swallow

I remember how the fruits of your sins
ripened inside me; made me a meadow of rotting
flesh

lips harsher than the rug burns on my
elbows harvested what little was left – I was a
corpse
limp and lifeless like a dead man's dick

but you were alive, feeding off my scraps that
lay scattered on the bottom bunk

I hope you are still plucking my skin from your
teeth
I hope I tasted like dog food left out in the heat
I hope you'll never forget me

Psych Ward Faces

Rebecca Gutteridge

The Rebel without a Cause

She was our unelected leader;
The Rebel.
The suicidal guru fixated
on knowledge and data;
she extracted numbers, birthdays, star signs
and judged us accordingly.
Stripes drawn on her legs,
she diagnosed herself a tiger.
We called ourselves the
Elementals - the Group
coursing with chemicals
prescribed by mad (never us) scientists.

On the ward that never lets you leave,
not really.

The Tyrant

Leather-clad, not-quite-five-foot-tall
true crime documentaries
blare through the modesty
curtain will me to scream,
murder blue murder!
As bodies decompose in beds around me.
A permanent resident; the tyrant
offered me juice
before her friendship was withdrawn.
Before she became my torment.

On the ward that never lets you leave,
not really.

The Evolution Of Katharina Henot (1570-1627)

Christina Hennemann

Call me patrician, postmaster,
the first woman to (fill in the gap).
Bishop circles truth, I was a wrong
rook pawn on the board, in the end-
game cornered and captured.

The nuns prayed for my wealth,
the bishop for my grace,
then they swore to my downfall,
the pact with the whores of power,
a spat in the palm, rub the book.

My lips were seals against the whip,
a bulwark against their battering,
and my neck had to crack
for the white king to win, I burned
and dissolved in the licking flames.

Purgation denied, paralysis inflicted,
I grew old enough to leave a legacy.
Panic ignited, paradox manifested,
three hundred years of slavering lies
like the fire freeing me from fear.

My name: a beam of light under the roof,
setting the letters on fire.

Me Too

Lisa Marie Serna

I finally felt beautiful,
to me. for me. Until...
you said we'd only get coffee
a well respected boy they said...
until you placed unconsented
hands on my chest forcing
unwanted embrace.
you said I was pretty
and you struck again.
whispering through the trembles
of your body
which imprisoned mine
and shuddering breaths
The sweat dripping from your
forehead and nose;
you smelled of death.
the ache in my thigh;
where you punched me
to stop kicking,
bruised and I counted the days
It took forever to fade.
I had been your prey...
-flashbacks-
I was young;
too young to process
any of what was going on
at eighteen,
I was seven again
maybe ten, maybe nine.
wishing the earth would

swallow me up that night.

We Bleed Art

Jillian Calahan

I am a woman.
Made of flesh and bone,
blood and art.
It flows from between my legs
splattered on the white canvas
that is my sheets.
At one time,
I would have felt ashamed.
I will no longer apologize
for being made of art.

Baby No. 3

Nat White

I don't know if baby number three was a boy or a girl... not that gender mattered, because we don't ever really know who our babies are, until they arrive and grow.

So no, I don't know what gender baby no.3 identified with, but the fact is, they existed - and I can't quite find the words to describe, how my heart doubled in size when the sonographer found a tiny little pod, with a tiny little pea inside, after they'd first said there wasn't anything but an empty shell.

As loud as a foghorn that same heart boasted its pride through my tongue, when I could finally show that black and white sonograph to everyone, especially the naysaying doctors, proving them 'wrong' that 'something was wrong'.

But oh, how desperately deep that same heart sunk when the first cramp began. When the spotting turned from pale pink to ruby red. My face draining to pasty white, a shade of dread to match my knuckles, that gripped his hand on the long drive to the hospital.
Oh, how that heart willingly succumbed, to the fear piercing it numb - the only word I can use to summarise, how it felt to lie on that bed. In that room. Full of people. Exposed. The contents of my

womb on show, oozing onto the blue and white plastic sheet placed beneath me.

Numb. Was how it felt to see the doctor's hand wrapped in a bloody glove. Knowing the DNA of my child, made from love, was somewhere within the crimson mess, about to be discarded - its coffin a yellow box adorned not with flowers, but a black symbol of toxic waste.

I can't quite tell you how I felt each time I went to the bathroom thereafter, to check and gather into a plastic container anything that resembled 'foetal tissue'. (Because this you see, was the only way they could possibly tell me whether it was an act of nature or a result of my own body's inadequacies.)

I can't quite explain how it felt when they told me a week later, that there was still 'something' growing inside of me. How my heart awoke, peeking back up like a submarine telescope - in a brief error of hope. Shrinking rapidly to the bottomless depths of grief, as they advised our little one couldn't possibly survive and they needed to 'make sure'. For if I continued to keep the pregnancy alive, they were certain that the condition of what I would eventually 'give birth to', was likely not anything that resembled, a child.

I can't quite express, how mortified and panic-stricken I felt as they suited up in their 'personal protective equipment' ready to inject me with a substance designed to chemically cease the growth of the cells containing their father's chromosomes - and mine.

But I can tell you...

When I got home, I lay on the Couch, for two whole days, watching every episode of 'Sex and the City' until I got to the one that had Charlotte's first loss and that, was the first time I really cried. Then the tears ... well after that they wouldn't subside. (Not, for a very long time.)

I can say, you can judge me all you like, but no one will ever know exactly how I feel inside. Nor the ins and outs of other women like me, who have come to this decision, faced with their own impossibilities.

I can tell you, on paper I had a 'chemically induced abortion', but in my heart, I was every bit acting in what I felt was the best interests of that life, like a mother should and would.

I can tell you that child would have been sixteen this year and if they were a girl she would have been called Grace.. and she.... he... they ... hold a place, that no one else can take.

I can tell you most wouldn't know until now, that when people ask me how many children I have, I say four... even though in my head I hear 'five'. And this, this part of me, I share with you, not for show and tell, but rather to join my sisterhood and yell from my side of the world, that the restrictions being imposed on women's rights are

NOT OK. We should not remain silent nor hang our heads in shame.

I did what was right for me, my body, my child and my family at the time, faced with circumstances of the same, I would go through it all again.

What kind of sick world is this becoming, where anyone is even willing to contemplate the possibility that women could be forced to breathe and grow life into the seeds forcefully inseminated by the loins of their rapists? Forced to deliver then give up a part of their soul or have it taken away, because they can't provide a safe or stable place for them to stay?

What kind of humanity is this, that creates laws that risk the health and wellbeing of the ones they say they are trying to protect? Opening the doors for them to end up part of a system of suffering, under government care, without mothers or fathers or family, at risk of abuse and neglect, born with disabilities, addictions, deformities...

And yes, this is a debate that has been going on for a very long time and I was initially a little late to stand with my fellow women of the world as we shake our fists and hang our heads and clasp our chests in disbelief.
Truthfully? I was building up some bravery. Simultaneously battling the nauseating reality that a country that prides itself on being forward-thinking could take such a dive backwards... to even contemplate making such archaic decisions for which they do not live with the consequences.

So much for 'keeping women safe'.

This may sound sexist as hell and I realise there's
a chance some may disagree, but it seems to me, if
the only ones signing off on these laws were born
with wombs, the majority would be retaining,
their right - to choose.

Body

Mimi Flood

My body is a political playground.
My body is hot when fingered.
My body is cool when you rub my breast.
My body rots
My body is throwaway behind a dump or a river.
My body is a product.
My body is a used condom.
My body is for a fuck.
My body is bruised.
My body is a whore, a slut.
My body is fat.
My body is raped.
My body is dog bait.
My body has bad skin
My body bleeds.
When I scream it sounds like a lullaby to them.

Ceridwen And The Cauldron Of Awen

After Sylvia Plath

Christina Hennemann

She is the eye of the word, fierce and
ambidextrous.
The lakes of the word are deep. The eye is green.
Mars hollers his moons on her breasts like muses
on speed,
crushing her forehead and whispering of
meritocracy.
Wispy, poetic stars watch over this land.
Severed from her skies by the ink of Rogue waves.
She pulls poems from the ivy-twined cauldron.

The earth is no cushion. It is a force to be
reckoned with,
sharp as a knife and silvery gleam.
It bends the trees in the storm like martial law; it
is brutal
in the outcry of last warning. She rules here.
Once a month the moon frightens the night—
twenty-nine torches lighting the path to Rebirth,
at its height she masterly moves tides and
dreams.

The cauldron of Awen bubbles up, it has a
pregnant shape.
The womb wriggles around and finds the earth.
The earth is her daughter. She is not fair like
Creirwy.

Her green gowns release hideous sons and
soothsaying poets.
How she enchants to unravel and knot—
the lap of poesy, licked by blazing flames,
bearing, from Ceridwen herself, its wild wombs.

Ceridwen has risen a high tide. Waves are wolfing
green and magical under the eyes of the sky.
Inside the poems, the words will all be green,
carving with their sharp tongues over the blank
pages,
their blades and knobs glowing with urgency.
The earth sees all of this. It is hurt and strong.
And the message of Awen's cauldron is vastness—
vastness and voice.

Coven

Eleanore Christine

They burnt and hung our ancestors
for possessing a power they did not understand
we the daughters of Eve, snake-whispered women
apple-bitten and cursed.

They have always sought to purge
the different, the strange
the marginalized, the misunderstood.

I see the same war being waged today
for the same religious agenda
by the same conservative old white men.

But the battlefield has changed:
now, the generals are politicians and judges
bans wielded like weapons instead of pyres and
rope
new laws written in ink and blood.

Choice is the devil that they fear
abortion our black magic
birth control a potion we consume
to poison our wombs.

They might have hunted me back then, too
for being unmarried, unmothered to a child
untethered to convention
for daring to be a woman who stands alone
for daring to be a woman.

Well, let me be damned for it
let me go up in ashes and smoke –

and let them hear the sound of me laughing
down below in hell.

Ripples

Sara Sabharwal

I want to be so full of love,
It spills into everything I do.
Even a small pebble
Makes ripples felt across the entire lake.
The world will feel my earthquake
As I spring forth from toxic soil,
A shining beacon of better days
Turning my face toward the sun,
Planting seeds of hope.
There will be storms,
There will be draughts,
But I know without a doubt
There will be beauty
In the strength and resiliency
Of millions of blooming petals unfurling
Proving that self love is the balm
That soothes the souls for generations
Of women.
Their voices echo in the eternity of my being.
I will be the link that breaks the chain
The storms I weather,
Cleanses the soil of my soul
So that one day
All my flowers will be kissed by the sun,
But know that their roots are deep
Wound together with the strength
Of their ancestors
Strong women
Wild women
Magic women

With blood of rubies
And bones of stardust.
The world burned their stories
Buried them deep in this earth
Forgetting they were seeds
That give birth to new generations
Of warriors
Fighting until it was safe to rest
Now I will try my best to be the healer.
Let my life's work be the elixir
That starts to heal generations
Of pain
So that my daughters can go forth
And create a new world.